99 WAYS TO ENRICH STRUGGLING BRAINS

DR DHEERAJ MEHROTRA

Contents

PREFACE

99 Ways To Enrich Struggling Brains *defines the development of new technologies, and the accumulation of academic knowledge has led to the discovery of alternative teaching strategies that may be more effective for the wide range of student learning styles.*

This strategy, known as brain-based learning, encourages pupils to be physically active as they study. In addition, Learning via sustained effort, or "productive struggle," fosters resilience and original thought. I am sure the book shall reflect and assist educators in making learning a priority for the kids.

Happy Learning.

www.authordheerajmehrotra.com

I
Ways to Enrich Struggling Brains

Use coloured chalk to do: Putting something on the blackboard/ whiteboard.

Could you kindly tell us something fresh, ma'am? This information is already included in the book. This is the response to any subject-related conversations taking place in classrooms throughout the world right now. Many people have been taken aback by the fact that "Walls" and "Friend Requests" have proven to be more popular than "Hello" or "Hi."

Are you and I thinking the same thing? It is up to us to decide whether or not to seize the opportunity to improve our working conditions, our level of service to customers, our sense of pride and dignity, and most importantly, our ability to satisfy the requirements necessary for the growth of our educational institutions. The marketing slogans support the instructors' pride to the best of their ability, but now in the new position of having a virtual presence.

The demand for intelligent and technologically savvy requisites in today's classrooms is a reflection of the changing nature of the teaching profession. The presence of a high-quality infrastructure at the learning environment, which would otherwise be of no value and is conducive to the development of young minds, is one of the best indicators of educational quality.

The parents are requested to make their selections for admission today in the majority of the mushrooming shops all around the country, much like any other service industry, with the option to have a tour around the School, the classes, and even they are told to leave their wards in the class as a trial run for them to decide of taste. This is similar to the way that any other service industry operates.

Also, consider the possibility of WHITE Boards and Colored Boards Markers being used as a habit. The seeds that are watered regularly take roots and thrive.

When we nurture seeds of joy in our children, it will cultivate a rich harvest of nurturing relationships and deep, loving bonds with them.

We are constantly watering the seeds of our children around us, with every look, word, expression and touch of ours. And what we focus on will grow.

Dress like a professional and use a GOOD PEN. Don't hang anything.
a Regular PEN as a Beauty Product Effect!

"No talking boys and girls" may no longer be the most prevalent terminology for instructors due to changing learner needs. Explore the power of participation in classrooms and the narration to study the cyber world connection with teachers in reality. No wonder you give a youngster an essay as homework; he/she will download it to deliver the next day, making you baffle the other students in line. Parents frequently view this as a threat because of the difficult effort they must perform to survive.

Think about learning and not TEACHING!

Don't forget that you are a TEACHER first, then a MATH, a PHYSICS, or ANY TEACHER OF A SUBJECT! And keep your drive.

ༀ

Let the kids do their work in partnership in a two-person group.
For every answer, put the two figures out what the answer is.
Collaboration makes 1 and 1 eleven!
For every job and project, even questions from the Teacher!

ༀ

Make ANCHOR charts to ADD FLAVOR to your classroom.

*Utilize an EDUCATIONAL TOOL
every time in class.*

જી

*Consider the recent case
to explain the concept, you are
using as a subject.*

જી

*Take pride in everything you do.
Deliver. Teachers must meet standards to the best of
their ability and interest. They need SMART teaching
choices to make learning enjoyable for kids. This
strategy teaches every youngster in the country how
to scale people, processes, and technology. The focus is
on establishing innovative institutional capabilities
and performance.*

જી

Build up your self-confidence.
First time - Always!

☙

*Deliver passion and WOW element
when TEACHING and LECTURING*

ജ

*Praise your CHILDREN in PUBLIC
all the time-2
Criticize them in PRIVATE if you must.
Ever happen too!*

ജ

*Give out the Information
with references/examples and
Coverage of facts in real-time.*

ജ

Share at least once a week.
ONE LEARNING LINK from the
a day with your kids.

Tell a story or give a report.
what would get them to read
your eyeballs.

രു

Always have a question in mind.
list of things to ask from your
Students!

രു

Greetings in the morning with
a personal touch like "Hi Ashish,
how are things?
Using the first name brings
Making friends and getting along.

*Discuss with your class
how your classroom works.
Give students control,
responsible for their own
success.*

*Innovations in the classroom
time and time again. Learning Happen
a hobby for kids that involves TOOLS
interesting and used often.*

Set up a set of classroom rules.
Courtesy Rules
Let all of the students do as
same.

Don't act disrespectfully.
Listen carefully to all the
There are kids in the class.

A classroom must be a place for
education that is the best. If you
showing students kindness and respect
if they have enough money,
walls to help you.

Think about a Room Makeover!
We no longer have to
think about having ROWS and
COLUMNS. There should be a circle,
Face-to-Face, Semi Circular

*where seating is set up
there is no one in the back at all.*

ॐ

*Reach out to the people
Children before their brains. Get
connected to them emotionally.
Make them strong in their feelings.*

*Cultivate your engagement
metre with students in the
class. Make sure that all of the kids
know you well and have talked to you at
at least one of your questions.
Each week!*

℘

*Use the strategy of
BRAINSTORMING
To figure out how to learn better using
the method of learning in a group.*

℘

*NLP techniques can help.
in school rooms like RAPPORT*

Building/Mirroring/Matching/ Anchoring and Visualization.

ॐ

Use
MIND MAPS
To teach the work and check it over done.

ॐ

Talk to the students.
encourage them, and direct their
writing ON THE SPOT!

ॐ

Teach people about self-awareness.
Knowledge. Create a consistent
Class schedule.

ॐ

Make it a habit to explain
instead of a right-based culture,
answer.

ॐ

*Use strategies for asking questions that
make all students
THINK & RESPOND*

ଔ

*Create the "WOW" moment
in the classroom studying/
teaching how to get people's attention
people watching. Deliver PRIDE &
DELIGHT!*

౭౦

*Use different approaches to
focus on students who don't behave.
Respect and acknowledge each
child's interest and attention.*

*Every school has digital classrooms, but does that
address the problem? My experience doubts. The
instructors' and educators' mindsets must be well-
functioning.*

The Teacher must be a TRAINER/LEARNER/ALL ROUNDER in CYBER SPACE. No EMAIL ID and MS OFFICE competence, but more... Having a WEBSITE, BLOG, WiKi, etc., and being SOCIALLY NETWORKED 24x7. Teachers love YouTube, TED, WatchKnowLearn, or any Ready Recknoner Web Content with Quality and Cream.

ജ

Don't try to teach hard.
Smartly teach.
Be a Smart Teacher on the Street!
Teach them the way they don't want to learn you like!

ജ

Find out about the march
of time with knowledge not
in general, not just about your subject.
Don't forget you are a TEACHER first.
then an English, Math, or Physics class or
a person who teaches Hindi.

ಊ

Teachers who do a good job must have
one world plan for a living!
IMPROVE
Check to see when you last taught.
...and the change you made
back then!

ಊ

Good teachers need to have
a one-word plan for life:
VISION

To give
DELIGHT THEIR STUDENTS!

Try to summarise 3Ks'
KODO, KAGENE, and KAIZEN
The Japanese way of thinking
thinking, acting, and getting better.
Continuously.

Make a cloud presence for yourself.
and make sure that you have google
to make an impression on your audience
time and time again. Participate in
professional and social sites.

The fact lies in the teacher being an innovator of traits and essence to explore the attention in the classroom.

The priority of taking Education and technology as a means to go together and it laminates with the questions in our minds viz. Should we do more, less? What about virtual schools?

Interactive white boards? Smartphones? Facebook and Twitter? Should kids be using internet? Should kids choose what they learn on internet? are legitimate conversations, and each person has to make these kinds of decisions based on their own comfort levels and according to the needs of the individual student.

*Bring your classrooms up to
the power to move to the next higher orbit
the TECHNOLOGY.
Make online blogs for students
to talk about the day's events.
What was learned, and how did it go?*

ജ

Commence your lesson on an

*note that it is exciting and full of energy
by continually pushing the
students and pique their interest
one of them.*

☙

*Tell them the learning goal.
The youngsters. Likewise, try to know
well of what students do
are aware of. applaud them for
their skill and respect
them because they are brilliant!*

☙

Always have some warm-ups
before starting to teach. This could
moving around the classroom,
as if you were to ask each kid in the class
go and shake hands with the
order of the very next plus-two roll
in any case!

Explore with e-learning.
or deliver some video on
AWARENESS *or* MOTIVATION
and talk about it in the
classroom.

Appreciate everything you have.
Better in the class.
Hey, I'm glad to be here at
the school. Every one of my students is the
The best kids in the world!
I want you all to get a perfect score.
In my topic!

ಐ

Put your ego aside.
Get ready to come down to the
students are at.

The teachers are no longer the sole imparters of
knowledge but they need to empower the students to
learn at pace and at their leisure through personal
learning networks keeping their special traits of
talents and interests.

The teachers just don't end up after the class is over
but on the jolt for 24 hours around the cyber linkage
or social networks further.

There is no wall now or the boundary of learning. The innovative educator has to evolve a personal learning network for his or her improvement first.

ೞ

Be friendly and polite.
Have a friendly attitude and
treat every student in your class well
as a VIP!

ೞ

Close the digital divide by
sharing with the students
studying how to use technology.
Don't be afraid to ask about technology.
if you need any IT skills from
those kids.

ೞ

Use the here and now.
Through CLOUD
Specific websites like
Scribd.com
Webs.com
Instagram
Podcast
Blog it
Linkedin
Add Twitter to your Facebook.
Presence!

Think about how you feel.
Keep drinking water, and don't miss
your meals as well as your work.
request to stand for too long
when they teach.

ം

Don't make funny faces when going for
arrangement classes/Substitute
classes don't use it as an
chance to learn from your mistakes.
students and apply what they've learned
as ICE BREATHERS for a normal
routine.

ം

Try to have high standards for every student. They will say, "All students deserve 100% in my subject."

Be organised and ready to go with the content, the flow, and the chapter every class has to talk about. Never go somewhere unprepared.

Build a GOOD relationship. with the students: A far ahead than counting people and time wish to interact.

*Carry your bottle of water,
book of activities and markers
if it were necessary to find the best
a lot of times, when TEACHING
without being interrupted.
Classroom.*

☙

*Keep some candy on hand for surprises.
as a reward for the students
worthy of a celebration or moment if
any.*

☙

*Make sure to sing "Happy Birthday."
SONGWRITER for the student in class
to play with the other kids.
It works wonders!*

Change the wall at random.
notices/charts/hangings and
teaching tools in the
in classrooms to get
learning through
NEW BUCKET LIST.

Be an AWESOME teacher
by keeping in mind the names of
every student in the class, by
FIRST NAME only, never address
them by the ROLL NUMBERS
or Sir Names.

Visit your home with a previous appointment at least once a SESSION to learn more about the child's ways of learning.

છ

Make sure you teach SKILLS FOR LIFE.

*too, as well as the SUBJECT
you are responsible for. It would
generate a special rapport of
share theirs with your students. May
require "Talking about MALA
and Obama to keep people's attention
one of them."*

*Wear any PERFUME you like,
be a RESPECTFUL PERSON
with some self-promotion
for students' love Street Smart
Teachers! Motivated, differentiated, relevant teachers
who leave no kid behind are crucial. Students enjoy
the topic only when they like the instructor, thus they
are directly proportional.*

*The teacher's passion in class with vocabulary is
shown through studying together rather than
instructing.*

*ALWAYS MENTION SOMETHING
BOOKS, and don't limit yourself to
the ones that are required,
e-books and references on the web.*

*Do not limit yourself to
Praising words and comments
viz. CAN DO BETTER can't be used.
the only ONLY comment/feedback
for the Grade Reports... PLEASE.*

*As a CLASS TEACHER dwell
some new ideas while doing
attendance. Don't close a limited
proxy or a coded answer of YES
SIR or PRESENT, SIR. Make some
Put up signs to make it loud
and open.*

*Ask questions for which 90% of the
students MAY answer not OTHER
The most important thing is not to
embrace PHOBIA but a CONNECT.*

*Activating a student oriented rather than a task
oriented classroom requires more of a connect, a
relationship with the student.*

Do QUALITY CIRCLE
way of teaching in the classroom with
at least 5 people in a
group. They have to sit down all.
and come up with ideas and
settle with DATA and then a.
The group gave a presentation.

✤

Encourage EXPERIENTIALly
KNOWLEDGE in almost all subjects
taught to make learning a part
of Soft Skills, making decisions
and get in touch with nature

✤

Make sure the BODY is right
It must be well-written.
spelt out so that it doesn't

if you send any terrible messages to the students. Students look at even the NAIL PAINT on the teachers!

ಙ

A TEACHER must honour DIFFERENT OPINIONS on the there are in the class. Every kid is essential to the style and deserves recognition.

ಙ

Be an AWESOME TEACHER TECHNOLOGY in classrooms to link up students 24x7. Take advantage of your PEN DRIVE. More often. Check out the link by EDUCATIONAL APPS

With your clients/audience!

☙

Think highly of your students.
They can also do great things by themselves.
Recognition and motivation from
your end. Consider them YOUNG.
NO LONGER KIDS, but NOW ADULTS!

☙

Treat your Students like your
real BOSSES out there. Remember
you must meet more than 40x5
sections equal 200 bosses each day.
Show them off with your
thought, knowledge, and
style, once and for all!

☙

*Explore LEARNING TOGETHER
not TEACHING and making sure to
you teach the lesson to a
hobby to learn about PLEASURE while
Share and learn.
Use the phrase "Let's Learn."
instead of saying, "Let me TEACH!"*

*Don't use the words too much.
"BUT," "TRY," and "IF"
during your sessions in
classroom
as they carry
NEGATIVE BELIEF!*

Use references, such as books by
to stay away from students'
appearance of
Sir, it's in the book already.
Use a new idea!

The teachers who motivate, differentiate, make
content relevant and leave no student behind are more
important than any other factor in particular. For
students like the subject only when they like the
teacher and is hence a directly proportional element
within a classroom.

Make a GOAL CHART for
the success of your students and
putting customer satisfaction first.
Assure all your students' score
One hundred per cent in your field!

Adjust how you act and
teaching skills now and then
by changing your ICE BREAKERS
plans and interactions
vocabulary. Activating a student oriented rather than
a task oriented classroom requires more of a connect,
a relationship with the student.

At times apologizing to students is a learning
moment. If we want kids with character, we must
model it to them with others as character counts.

❧

Be aware and awake!
You must all be looking at the
backs of your Heads!
Ask your students to work together,
and think about your class's
Facebook Page!

❧

*Pay close attention and return to
their questions! Activating a student-oriented
classroom as opposed to a task-oriented classroom
necessitates more of a connection, a relationship with
the student. Sometimes apologising to pupils is a
teaching opportunity. If we want our children to have
character, we must show them by example.*

*The experiences all agree that a genuine apology
includes honestly admitting wrong, totally taking
responsibility, a humbled plea for forgiveness,
instantly altering behaviour, and, most importantly,
aggressively restoring trust.*

*Rather than giving book contents, a dosage of
eagerness to seek information is wanted. When
students appear to be information crusaders, teachers
must behave as facilitators more than stern
disciplinarians.*

Think about the win-win scenario.
And WISDOM OF OWNERSHIP. My boys
Girls are the best, too.
For winners, they MAKE it happen.
losers, let it HAPPEN!

໋

Don't compare and point the
other teachers for their work in
public; the more you are to blame.
The more boring you get!

໋

Accept that you aren't perfect.
Have a bad habit you want to change?
Time goes on. Forget your yester
when you were a student, you can
but not what you were taught!

The students today are no longer kids but young adults and hence need recognition as individuals and partnership in the learning process.

৪৩

Admit you are NOT PERFECT
Focus on learning how to learn.
rather than just once in a while
occurrence!

৪৩

Look into the
KWINK Analysis
(Knowing What I Now Know)
and try manipulating your
problems and Good points.
Focus on your weaknesses to
use them as your builders
for betterment.

৪৩

Ignore the
COMFORT ZONE
Accept difficulties and the
ways to teach others.
subjects/senior classes/
putting together chances/
involvement and other
assignments as a pride!

&

*Accept 100% responsibility
for both your grade and the
how your class is doing academically.
This is the way to boost your self-esteem,
self-confidence and reliance on oneself
respect for oneself.*

଼

*Think happy thoughts with
students and coworkers
ALL THE TIME
This will make you smarter.
self and rapport among your
peers. Make wanting to learn a top priority instead of
an occasional thing.*

*Also, teachers should make getting rid of ignorance
the main goal of every interaction with students,
other teachers, peers, and parents.*

The most important thing to remember is that it's never too late to get better.

Part of reality is interacting with the kids in class without fear, but with closeness and a sense of pride from both the kids and the teachers as a whole.

To the facts, fear kills dreams more than failure ever will, and this is something that everyone should focus on first.

છ૭

Explore classroom management skills through setting your priorities using the 80/20 rule to your daily tasks and activities. Remember that 80 per cent of your results will come from 20 per cent of the items on your list. Get your classroom event on your students' calendars by creating a Facebook Event.

છ૭

*Minimize your distractions within
the classrooms. Avoid checking
messages/calls/posts/updates
while in your classroom. A ready
reckoner student-friendly
the teacher does not even carry a
mobile phones in the classroom
ever.*

*Act like a ZEN MASTER, not a
RING MASTER
Let the students in the class
follow your spiritual learning
and Blessings instead of being a HARD
TASK MASTER.*

Be SMART!
Systematic: In teaching
Meticulous: In Working
Artistic: In the Presentation
Realistic: In Calibration
Tactful: In Classroom
Management

Calibrate your behaviour as per

*the scenario of the classroom
situation. Never carry a grudge
or a disliking for any student
ever. Forgive and Forget with
some golden words like*
*May GOD Bless you! The wonderful words, do help our
children to use a wide range of wonderful words in
their writings. We must just not blame them of their
handwriting and knowledge limitation, instead, must
be the part and the parcel of their learning.*

*Also to create a rapport with the students, the
teaching tools in practice by the teachers need to be
evaluated with reference to the usage during the
lesson being appropriate or not. With this the
teacher's subject knowledge, enthusiasm, methods of
questioning, exposition and problem solving relate to
multilevel dimension for judging.*

*The teachers as facilitators explore and expose the
learning objectives in a big bang way via repartees
and the responses generated after every classes or via
the Parents' Teachers' Meetings on jolt and
achievements. Let us conclude the fact that children
will love and explore their presence in the classrooms
only when given the recognition of individual
concerns, it is mandatory for teachers to call the kids
by their first names keeping them at pace to
importance rather than experiencing the only preface
with them at the time of the roll calls and that too
with referencing through roll numbers.*

৵

Stop being responsive. Instead, protect your time and energy for the things that matter most. If you are finding an interesting discussion time, ask students to simply continue the discussion on Facebook and move on.

ॐ

*Incorporate a procedure of a
T-MAIL
(Teachers' Mail Box)
A note to the teacher on some query or an experience to share in private.*

ॐ

Use the POST-IT NOTES on classroom walls against a name. It can be praise or a personal improvement note for the child. Both the teacher to the child and vice-versa!

৪৩

Have a conversation Notebook with the students in circulation within the class. This may be a personal small notebook to the teacher by the kids with a special note on queries and achievements.

৪৩

Share

MORNING GREETINGS
On a personal note, during getting
together moments and during
the Assembly hours to develop
rapport with the students.

&

Share a meal with the students
during lunch hours and breaks.
The kids enjoy sharing the food
and love being praised on taste
and share the enjoyment for
trust and rapport building. In order to govern and
sense student's friendly classroom, the teachers need to
check on their share of the day, of some new
vocabulary and make a haze to the fact that the
students should be held accountable for the number
and the quality of questions students ask and pursue
during the teaching learning process.

Right from Good Morning Wishing to the, Thank you
children, the time and share has to be so friendly and
empowering so as to make them take home moments
of joy and some attributes to share with their parents.

This must be a priority.

For teachers need to showcase in action that they are not perfect and never will be.

• • •

They must take risks with their teaching and failing must be a part of the learning process. For we are facing the Google Generation which empowers self and is not a dependent lot on either the library or the teacher, fortunately or unfortunately, I doubt my words too. As teachers, we must make progress evident, alter grading processes, model desired habits, and avoid getting caught up in school, student, and parent politics.

About The Author

Dheeraj Mehrotra, MS, MPhil, PhD (Education Management) honoris causa., a white and a yellow belt in SIX SIGMA, a Certified NLP Business Diploma holder, is an Educational Innovator, Author, with expertise in Six Sigma In Education, Academic Audits, Neuro-Linguistic Programming (NLP), Total Quality Management In Education, an Experiential Educator, a CBSE Resource towards School Assessment (SQAA), CCE, JIT, Five S, and KAIZEN. He has authored over 100 books on topics which include Computer Science, AI, Digital Body Language, NLP, Quality Circles, School Management, Classroom Effectiveness and Safety and security in schools. A former Principal at De Indian Public School, New Delhi, (INDIA), NPS

International School, Guwahati, and Education Officer at GEMS, Gurgaon, with an ample teaching experience of over Two Decades, he is a certified Trainer for Quality Circles/ TQM in Education and QCI Standards for School Accreditation/ School Audits and Management. He has also been honoured with the President of India's National Teacher Award in the year 2006 and the Best Science Teacher State Award (By the Ministry of Science and Technology, State of UP), Innovation in Education for his inception of Six Sigma In Education by Education Watch, New Delhi and Education World- Best Teacher Award, BOLT Learner Teacher Award by Air India, 'Innovation in Education Award 2016' by Higher Education Forum (HEF), Gujarat Chapter, among others. He has developed over 150 FREE EDUCATIONAL MOBILE Apps for the Google Play Store exclusively for Teachers, Students, and Parents. This work has been recognised by the LIMCA BOOK OF RECORDS & INDIA BOOK OF RECORDS as the only Indian to draw that feast. Dr Mehrotra works as a PRINCIPAL at KUNWARS GLOBAL SCHOOL, Lucknow, in India. He has conducted over 1000 workshops globally on "Excellence In Education" integrated with Total Quality Management and Six Sigma, Technology Integration in Education (TIE), Developing towards being ROCKSTAR TEACHERS, including Cyberspace, Cyber Security, Classroom Management, School Leadership & Management, and Innovative teaching within classrooms via Mind Maps, NLP and Experiential Learning in Academics. He is an active TEDx speaker and can be viewed on the youtube TEDx channel.

As a premium UDEMY Instructor, he has developed over 450 courses and caters to over 8 Lakh students from 180 countries.

He can be visited at www.authordheerajmehrotra.com

PRIORITY LEARNING FOR EDUCATORS
It is worth knowing now!
digital
body
Language
WORK
ETHICS
FOR
TEACHERS
TEACHER'S
TOOLKIT
POST COVID
TOWARDS EXCELLENCE IN
TEACHING & LEARNING
200
WOW TEACHING
IDEAS
NLP
FOR TEACHERS
Towards Quality Teaching Skills
Teachers' Favourite
Teaching Strategies
That Work
Buy now at
amazon.in
APPLYING
SIX SIGMA
WITHIN
CLASSROOMS
DR. DHEERAJ MEHROTRA
EXPERIENTIAL
LEARNING
FOR
EDUCATORS
TOWARDS QUALITY LITERACY FOR ALL
Academic
Audits
In Schools
What, Why &
How?